ISAAC ASIMOV'S
Library of the Universe

URANUS:
The Sideways Planet

TreeHouse

1430 W. Susquehanna Ave
Philadelphia, PA 19121
215-236-1760 I treehousebooks.org

by Isaac Asimov

Gareth Stevens Children's Books
London • Milwaukee

A note from the editors: In the United States and other places — including this book — a billion is the number represented by 1 followed by nine zeros — 1,000,000,000. In other countries, including Britain, this number is often called 'a thousand million', and one billion would then be represented by 1 followed by 12 zeros— 1,000,000,000,000: a million million, which is called a 'trillion' in this book.

The reproduction rights to all photographs and illustrations in this book are controlled by the individuals or institutions credited on page 32 and may not be reproduced without their permission.

British Library Cataloguing in Publication Data

Asimov, Isaac, 1920-
    Uranus: the sideways planet.
    1. Uranus
    I. Title II. Series
    523.47

    ISBN 0-83687-010-7

A Gareth Stevens Children's Books edition

Edited, designed, and produced by
Gareth Stevens Children's Books   31 Newington Green, London N16 9PU

First published in the United States and Canada in 1988 by Gareth Stevens, Inc.
First published in the United Kingdom in 1989 by Gareth Stevens Children's Books

Cover painting © Julian Baum

Designer: Laurie Shock
Picture research: Kathy Keller
Artwork commissioning: Kathy Keller and Laurie Shock
Project editors: Mark Sachner and MaryLee Knowlton
Editor (UK): Dee Turner

Technical advisers and consulting editors: Greg Walz-Chojnacki and Julian Baum

1 2 3 4 5 6 7 8 9 9 93 92 91 90 89

CONTENTS

Introduction

We live in the Universe, an enormously large place. Only in the last 50 years or so have we found out how large it really is.

It's only natural that we should want to understand the place we live in, and in the last 50 years, we have developed new instruments with which to get such understanding. We have radio telescopes, satellites, probes, and many other things that have told us far more about the Universe than could possibly be imagined when I was young.

Nowadays, we have seen close-up views of planets. We have learned about quasars and pulsars, about black holes and supernovas. We have learned amazing facts about how the Universe may have come into being and how it may end. Nothing can be more astonishing and more interesting.

We have learned a great deal, for instance, about a planet that is over three billion km away from us. This planet is Uranus, which was named after the Greek god of the sky. Before 1986 we could only see it as a tiny spot of light through our telescopes. Now we have seen it up close and know much more about it and about the smaller objects that circle it.

This book tells you about that planet.

On January 25, 1986, Voyager 2 took this beautiful picture of Uranus from a distance of one million km. On its encounter with Uranus, Voyager discovered additional rings and 10 new moons.

A Strange Comet

The year: 1781. The place: Bath, England. The event: A German astronomer named William Herschel studying the sky with a telescope he built himself. On March 13, 1781, he sees a little spot of light where no such spot should be. He thinks it must be a comet, but it isn't fuzzy-looking, as comets usually are. It moves slowly, night by night, and Herschel soon realizes that it is circling the Sun far beyond the most distant planet then known, Saturn. Herschel realizes he has discovered a new, still more distant planet. All the other planets have been known since ancient times. This new planet is the first one to be discovered in modern times. Its name: Uranus.

Sir William Herschel, holding a pamphlet announcing his discovery of Uranus.

Built in 1789, Herschel's 12-m telescope was the largest in the world. In 1820, when Herschel became first president of England's Royal Astronomical Society, the telescope became the Society's emblem.

A Small Giant

What have we learned about this modern planet? Well, even without the help of the Voyager 2 space probe, astronomers could work out Uranus' distance by watching its motion. It is 2,880,000,000 km from the Sun. That is 19 times as far from the Sun as Earth is. From the width of the little disc of light at that distance, its true size could be worked out. It is 51,000 km across, which is just four times the width of Earth. Uranus has a mass nearly 15 times that of Earth, so it is a giant planet. It is not nearly as large as Jupiter, though. Jupiter, the largest planet, is over 20 times as massive as Uranus.

Bode's Law: too good to be true!

In 1772, the astronomer Daniel Titius worked out a simple formula that showed how far each planet ought to be from the Sun. Another astronomer, Johann Bode, thought the formula was important and called it to everyone's attention. It was called 'Bode's Law' for that reason. By Bode's Law, a planet beyond Saturn ought to be about 2,880,000,000 km from the Sun. When Uranus was discovered in 1781, that proved to be its distance! Everyone was astonished. However, when Neptune, the next farther planet, was discovered, it didn't fit Bode's law. For that reason, astronomers abandoned the law as worthless.

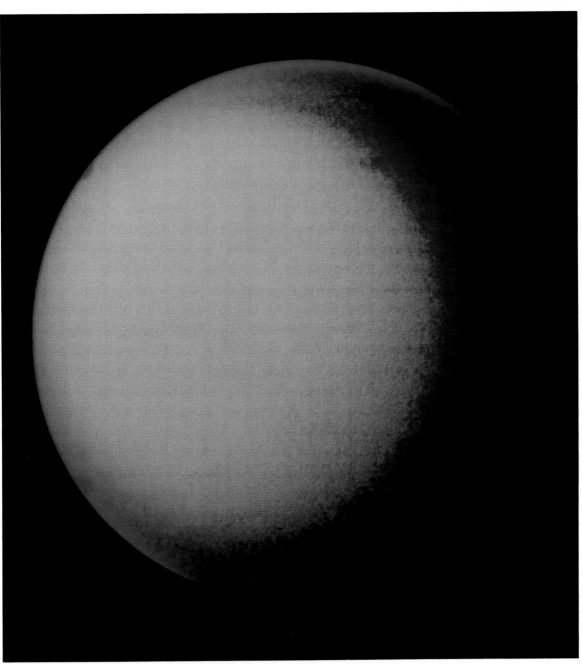

Special colour filters on Voyager 2's cameras show the hazes
produced by gases around Uranus.

A Peculiar Planet

Uranus is so far away that for about 200 years scientists could not make out how quickly it turns on its axis. They could tell there was something odd about the turning, though. Most planets turn on their axis in such a way that they are almost upright as they move about the Sun. Earth's axis is tipped only one-quarter of the way from the vertical. Uranus' axis, however, is tipped so far that it seems to be lying on its side as it moves around the Sun. It is the only planet with an axis tipped that way, so that some think of it as a sideways planet.

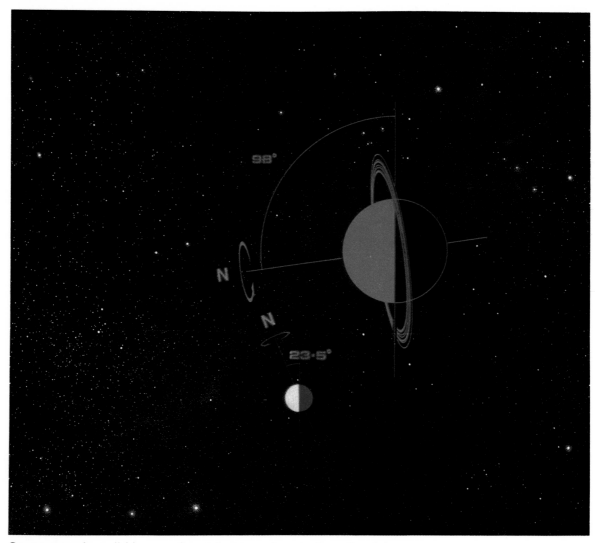

Some people call Uranus the sideways planet since it rotates over 90° from the vertical. Earth, as you can see, is only slightly tilted in its rotation.

8

Planetesimals bouncing around and colliding with a newly formed planet may have affected that planet's tilt. Here, two planetesimals collide and fragment into smaller planetesimals.

Why does Uranus rotate on its side?

Here is one possible reason: When the planets formed, a lot of smaller bits of matter, called planetesimals, came together. When the planet was almost formed, the last few planetesimals that banged into it would upset it a little. Of course, the planetesimals came from every direction, so all the tilts evened out. It may have been that Uranus just happened to be hit, at the last minute, by some large planetesimals all from the same direction. That would create a big tilt that never got straightened out. That is just a theory, however. We don't really know.

Uranus' Family of Moons

Like most planets, Uranus has its own natural satellites, or moons. These are smaller worlds that circle Uranus — just as our Moon circles the Earth. Two were discovered by Herschel himself in 1787. He named them Oberon and Titania, after the king and queen of fairies in Shakespeare's *A Midsummer Night's Dream*. Two more were discovered 64 years later. They were named Ariel and Umbriel, after two other fairies in a poem by Alexander Pope.

Finally, in 1948, a fifth satellite was discovered and named Miranda, after the heroine of *The Tempest*, another of Shakespeare's plays. Their orbits around Uranus are tipped just as the planet's axis is. From Earth, these moons seem to go up and down, not side to side, as other planets' moons do. Was this the full count of moons for Uranus, or would more be found?

Here are the largest moons of Uranus. From top to bottom: Miranda, Ariel, Umbriel, Titania, and Oberon. They are all named after characters in classic English literature. This composite photo shows how big these satellites are in relation to one another. Titania and Oberon are clearly the largest — and nearly the same size. Titania's diameter is about 1,594 km; Oberon's is about 1,564 km.

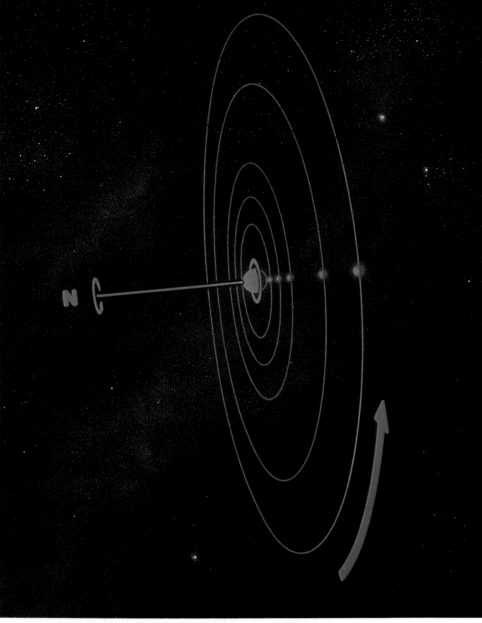

The major moons of Uranus in 'sideways' orbit around their parent planet. From outermost to closest, they are Oberon, Titania, Umbriel, Ariel, and Miranda. Note how nicely their orbits parallel not only each other but also Uranus' rings.

Introducing . . . the planet Herschel?

When Uranus was discovered, Herschel wanted to call it Georgium Sidus (Latin for 'George's Star') in honour of George III, the British king. Other British astronomers wanted to call it 'Herschel' in honour of its discoverer. But astronomers elsewhere in Europe wanted a name out of mythology, not out of England! Here is how they figured it: Going out from Earth, there is Mars. Then there is Jupiter, who is Mars' father in the myths; then Saturn, who is Jupiter's father. So they called the new planet Uranus, after Saturn's father.

Surprise: Ringed Planet!

In 1977, Uranus moved in front of a dim star. Astronomers watched closely because they wanted to measure how the star light dimmed as Uranus' atmosphere passed in front of it. That would tell them something about the atmosphere. To their surprise, the star blinked out several times <u>before</u> the atmosphere moved in front of it. It blinked out again, several times, after Uranus and its atmosphere had moved away. They decided Uranus had several rings of matter circling it, just as Saturn has. Saturn's rings are huge and bright, but Uranus' are very thin and dark.

The quiet giant

All the planets known from ancient times are bright and move in the sky from one night to the next. This attracts our attention. But Uranus is much farther away. Therefore, it is much dimmer, and it moves more slowly than other planets do, so it attracts almost no attention. In 1690, an English astronomer, John Flamsteed, saw a dim star in the constellation Taurus. He called it '34 Taurii' and marked it on his starmap. It was actually Uranus. If Flamsteed had gone back to look at it a few nights later, he would have seen that it had moved. So you see, Uranus was <u>seen</u> 91 years before it was <u>discovered</u>.

Left: As scientists were waiting to watch Uranus pass in front of a star, the star 'blinked' off and on five times — <u>before</u> the planet blocked the star. When the star blinked off and on five times <u>after</u> the planet blocked the star, the scientists knew they had discovered that Uranus had rings.

13

Closing in on Uranus: This photo of Uranus was taken by Voyager 2 from 247 million km away, on July 15, 1985 — six months before the January 25, 1986, flyby. This was the first real chance for scientists to see the relation of the planet to its moons. In this composite picture, several of the moons can be seen.

A Distant Puzzle

Astronomers were excited by the surprising discovery of rings around Uranus. But it didn't seem as though we would ever find out more about Uranus. It was so far away that it just looked like a little bluish circle of light. Jupiter and Saturn, two planets that are closer and larger than Uranus, can be seen much more easily. In fact, these two giants show up in telescopes well enough for us to make out markings on the surface. Those markings move about the surface, and we can see how fast the planets rotate. But Uranus, small and dim, does not show markings, and it remained pretty much a puzzle for over 200 years.

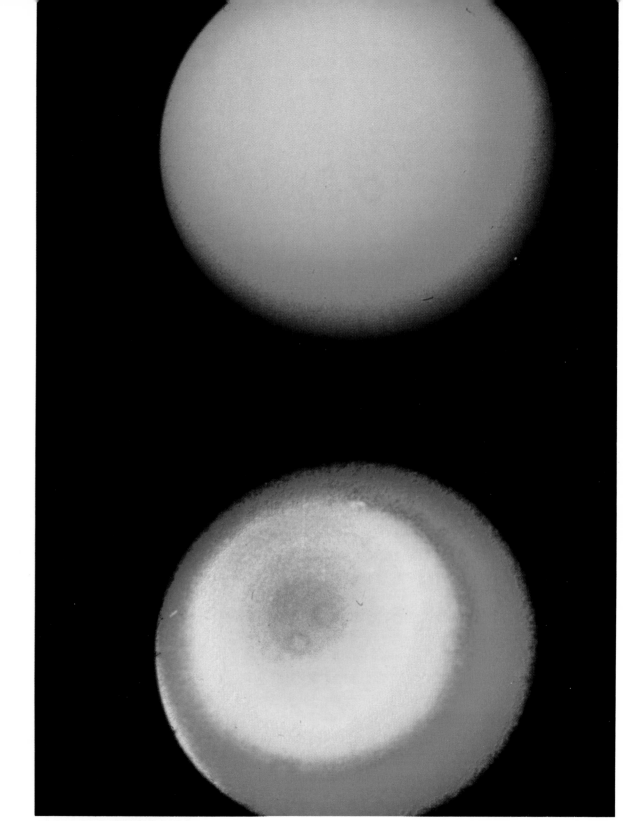

Two views of Uranus: The top picture shows how the planet would appear to a person in a spacecraft 18 million km from Uranus. The other picture is taken through colour filters and enhanced by computer to show the gases present on and around Uranus. In both shots, the view is toward the planet's pole of rotation, which lies just left of centre.

Voyager 2: Our Faithful Robot

But today we have learned far more about Uranus than we knew even as recently as the early 1980s — and in ways that astronomers like Herschel might not even have imagined. We have built space probes, and they have travelled out to the distant planets. Voyager 1 and Voyager 2 were sent into space in 1977. Both Voyager probes passed Jupiter and Saturn, taking photographs as they flew by. Voyager 2 had its course arranged so that it continued toward Uranus. It passed Uranus in January, 1986, and photographed it. This wasn't easy, because Uranus is so far from the Sun that it only gets 1/360th as much light as we do. Voyager 2 had to take pictures in this dim light as it was moving past, but it did a magnificent job after travelling through space for nine years.

Voyager 2 came closest to Uranus on January 24, 1986. On board the probe were 104 kg of scientific instruments. Some of them sent back many of the pictures in this book! After photographing Uranus, Voyager 2 headed off for its 1989 date with Neptune.

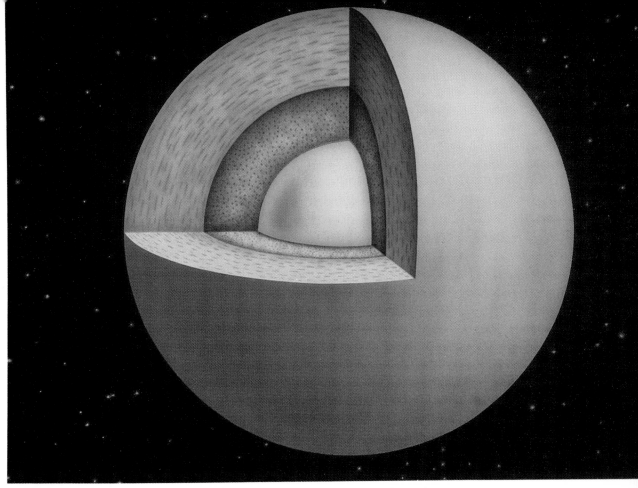

Landing on a gaseous planet like Uranus would be impossible, since the planet really has no land. This cutaway picture shows the planet's three layers: a centre of molten rock, surrounded by a layer of liquid, and an outer layer of gas.

And now that Voyager 2 has flown past Uranus, we know much more about this giant planet than we did only a few years ago. For example, we now know that Uranus may have a molten rock core that is 13,000 km across. This is about the size of Earth. This core is surrounded by an 8,000-km deep 'sea' made up mostly of water, and an 11,000-km thick atmosphere of helium and hydrogen. With so much of the planet made up of a gaseous atmosphere, Uranus is one of the gas giants — a group that includes Jupiter, Saturn, and Neptune.

The Misty Veil

Voyager 2's photographs were beamed back to Earth. They showed Uranus much more clearly than we can see it with a telescope from Earth, but it still turned out to be just a blue globe. Sunlight warms the atmospheres of Jupiter and Saturn, stirring the clouds into circles and belts. But Uranus receives so little sunlight that its atmosphere is much quieter. The Voyager scientists took special photos which revealed bright, thin clouds deep in the atmosphere. Radio signals also showed that it takes Uranus about 17 hours to turn on its axis. Until then, guesses had been anywhere from 10 to 25 hours.

Scientists were delighted that they could now compare the motions of the clouds to Uranus' spin, since that gives them important clues about the way weather works on Uranus.

Right: A Uranian cloud. This Voyager 2 picture shows a cloud along the limb, or bluish edge, of Uranus. The photo was taken through colour filters and enhanced by computer. In true colour, the cloud would have been nearly invisible.

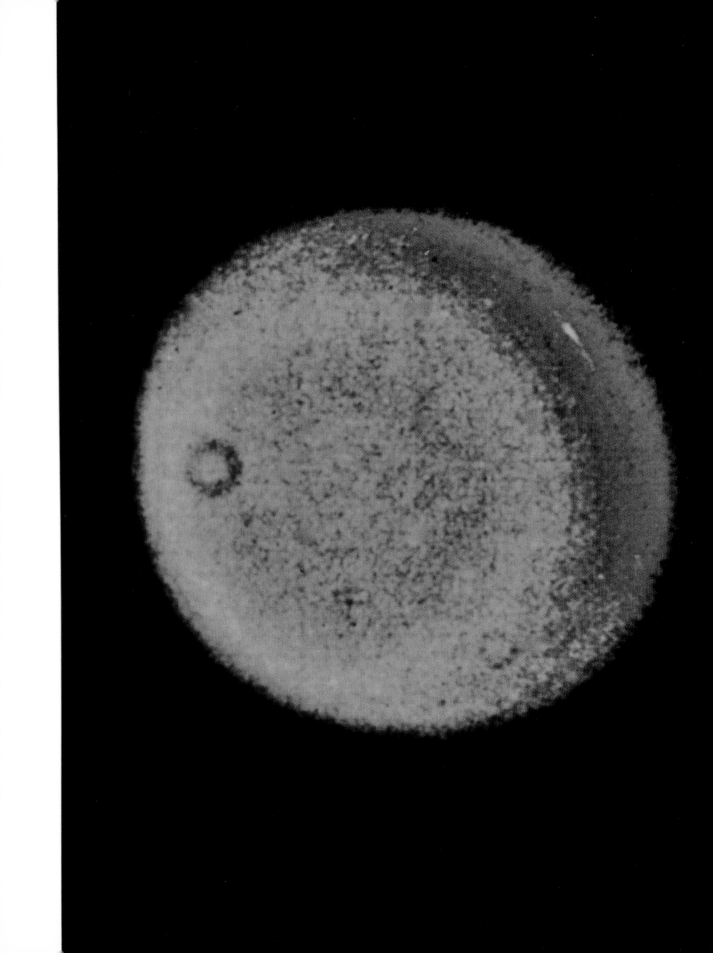

epsilon

delta
gamma
eta

beta

alpha

4
5
6

Nine of Uranus' rings. The variety of colour of the rings, here artificially enhanced, shows that they have different origins. They're really shades of grey, not different from one another to the human eye, but significantly different when seen through scientific instruments. The tenth ring, between epsilon and delta, is not clearly featured in this picture.

Close-up of the Rings and Moons of Uranus

Although Uranus' rings were detected from Earth, they weren't actually seen. Astronomers had noticed in 1977 that the rings blocked starlight when the planet moved in front of a star. But this was before Voyager came upon Uranus. Voyager 2 sent back photographs that actually showed the rings. So far, scientists have made out 11 separate dark rings around Uranus from these photographs. In addition, Voyager 2 detected more moons. We now know that Uranus has 15 moons, or satellites, in all. Miranda is the smallest moon of Uranus that we can see from Earth. It is about 480 km across, and it is the closest to Uranus. Voyager 2 spotted 10 more moons that are still closer to Uranus and even smaller than Miranda. The smallest is only 16 km across.

This combination of four photos of Ariel shows craters and valleys on the moon's surface. Though the surface temperature is now far lower than the melting point of water, scientists have found evidence that liquid once flowed on the surface, smoothing over many craters and cracks.

The Dark Moons of Uranus

So Uranus has many moons — 15 in all! But they are quite small. The five larger satellites of Uranus are not as large as the largest that circle Jupiter and Saturn. Jupiter has four satellites that are at least 3,200 km across, and Saturn has one. Neptune and even our small planet, Earth, each have a satellite that's more than 3,200 km across. But Uranus' largest satellite, Titania, is only 1,593 km across! We also know from Voyager 2 that Uranus' satellites are surprisingly dark — just like its rings. Umbriel is the darkest, and while it, like the others, has craters and other markings, Umbriel has a small white circle that looks like a powdered doughnut on a dark plate. Scientists think the circle might be the rim of a large, bright crater.

Ariel: Of Uranus' five large moons, Ariel is second closest to the planet. It has a cratered surface. Ariel has been reshaped by rock movements and displacements throughout its surface. In this illustration, Uranus looms large above.

Titania: The second farthest away of Uranus' five large moons, Titania has many visible impact craters as well as a major canyon formed by rock movements. In the cold, dark night, Uranus appears in a quarter phase.

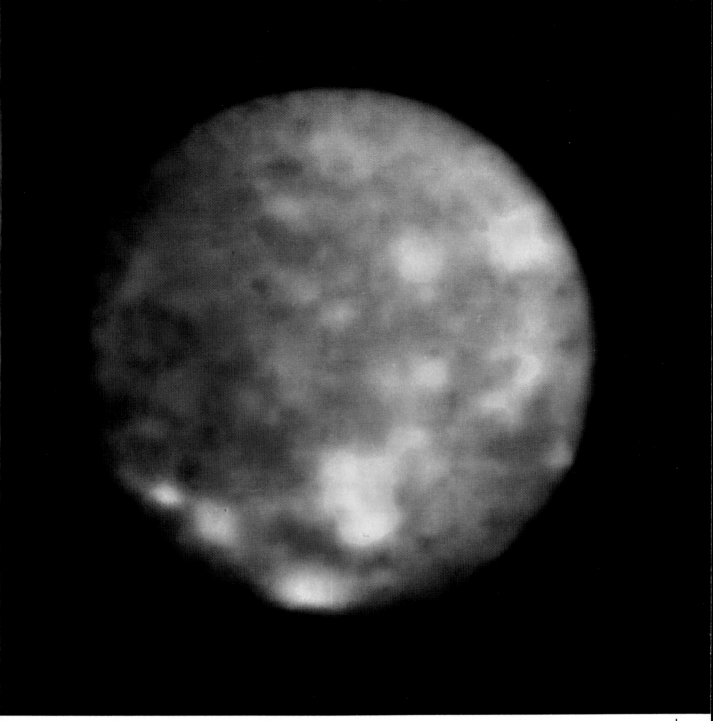

This photo of Titania shows areas of lighter and darker material. These are probably craters caused by bombarding cosmic debris. Though this picture was shot with orange and violet filters, it still shows the lack of colour that is typical of the moons and rings of Uranus.

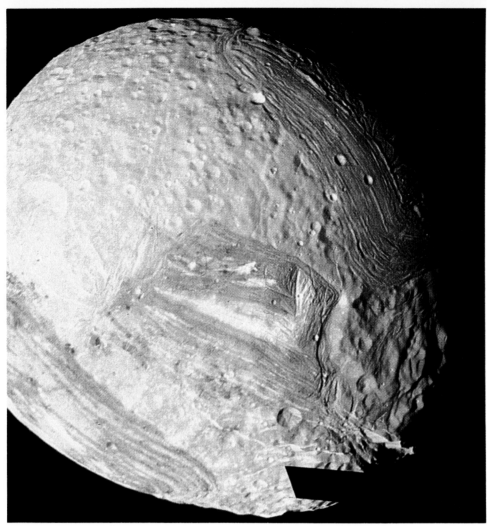

Of Uranus' five major moons, Miranda is the closest to its parent planet — and the smallest. It is only about 480 km in diameter. But it has a widely varying surface. Some of its cliffs, or scarps, are higher than those of the Grand Canyon in the United States.

Amazing Miranda

Of all the moons of Uranus, Miranda is the most surprising. It has all kinds of markings on it. It has canyons and grooves and parallel marks that look like a stack of pancakes seen on edge. It also has a bright marking that looks like a V. Scientists find it difficult to understand how all these markings were made. Some think that when Miranda was first formed it may have been struck by another body and the two broke up into smaller chunks. These chunks then came back together haphazardly to form the present Miranda.

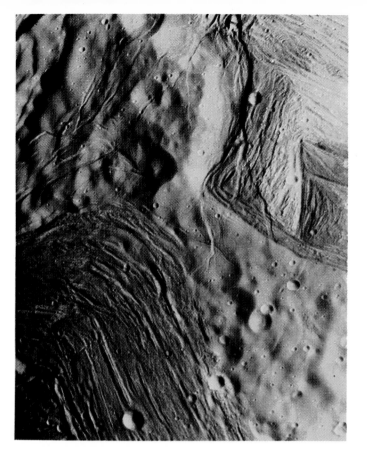

This Voyager 2 picture shows some of Miranda's distinctive features. Scarps and bowl-shaped craters are typical of moon terrain. But the V-shaped pattern is one of the more unusual features of this unusual moon.

Since gaseous Uranus would be impossible to land on, Miranda might provide our best Uranian base. Some day, a space probe like this one may send us more information about Uranus, its rings, and its moons.

See You in the Next Century!

The pictures sent back by Voyager 2 are all we've got so far if we want to study Uranus, its rings, and its satellites in detail. What's more, we won't have other pictures of this kind for a long time. It may be many years, perhaps even a century, before another probe is sent out to study Uranus. Of course, by the time a hundred years passes, we will have much more complicated probes that can study the planet in greater detail. Who knows? Perhaps the next probe will even carry human beings with it.

Another planet to be discovered?

When Uranus was first discovered, it didn't seem to follow the law of gravity exactly as it turned about the Sun. It seemed to lag a bit. Perhaps there was another large planet beyond it that had not yet been discovered. The gravitational pull of this more distant planet wasn't allowed for. If it <u>were</u> allowed for, that might account for Uranus' lag. The distant planet was looked for, found, and named Neptune. However, there is still a very small lag in Uranus' motion about the Sun that cannot be explained by the presence of either Neptune or tiny Pluto, which was discovered in 1930. Is there another large planet beyond Neptune? If so, it hasn't yet been found. If not, what causes that last bit of lag?

Could this child be a future relative of yours? He could be one of the first to travel to Uranus.

Fact File: Uranus

Uranus, the third largest planet and the seventh closest to the Sun, is also one of the most unusual. Its tipped axis means that each pole faces the Sun during half of Uranus' 84-year orbit. This means that each half of Uranus has a 42-year-long 'day' of sunlight followed by a 42-year-long 'night' of darkness.

Above: The Sun and its Solar system family, left to right: Mercury, Venus, Earth, Mars, Jupiter, Saturn, Uranus, Neptune, Pluto.

The Moons of Uranus		
Name	Diameter	Distance From Uranus' Centre
Miranda	298 miles (480 km)	80,402 miles (129,390 km)
Ariel	729 miles (1,174 km)	118,670 miles (191,020 km)
Umbriel	740 miles (1,192 km)	165,479 miles (266,300 km)
Titania	990 miles (1,594 km)	270,874 miles (435,910 km)
Oberon	961 miles (1,546 km)	362,599 miles (583,520 km)
1986U7	10 miles (16 km)	30,927 miles (49,770 km)
1986U8	15 miles (24 km)	33,431 miles (53,800 km)
1986U9	30 miles (48 km)	36,768 miles (59,170 km)
1986U3	50 miles (80 km)	38,390 miles (61,780 km)
1986U6	30 miles (48 km)	38,949 miles (62,680 km)
1986U2	50 miles (80 km)	39,987 miles (64,350 km)
1986U1	50 miles (80 km)	41,068 miles (66,090 km)
1986U4	30 miles (48 km)	43,461 miles (69,940 km)
1986U5	30 miles (48 km)	46,767 miles (75,260 km)
1985U1	105 miles (168 km)	53,440 miles (86,000 km)

Planet	Diameter
Uranus	31,567 miles (50,800 km)
Earth	7,927 miles (12,756 km)

The Sun and Its Family of Planets

Right: Here is a close-up of Uranus and its five major satellites (from top to bottom), Miranda, Ariel, Umbriel, Titania, and Oberon. Thanks to Voyager, we now know about 10 smaller moons orbiting even closer to Uranus within the orbit of Miranda.

Uranus: How It Measures Up to Earth

Rotation Period (length of day)	Period of Orbit Around Sun (length of year)	Known Moons	Surface Gravity	Distance from Sun (nearest-farthest)	Least Time It Takes for Light to Travel to Earth
17 hours, 18 minutes	365.25 days (84.0 years)	15	0.91*	1.7-1.9 billion miles (2.7-3 billion km)	2.5 hours
23 hours, 56 minutes	365.25 days (one year)	1	1.00*	92-95 million miles (147-152 million km)	—

* Multiply your weight by this number to find out how much you would weigh on this planet.

29

More Books About Uranus

Here are more books that contain information about Uranus. If you are interested in them, look for them in your library or bookshop.

Discovering Astronomy by Jacqueline and Simon Mitton (Longman, 1979)
Our Solar System by Isaac Asimov (Gareth Stevens, 1989)
Planets by N. S. Barrett (Franklin Watts, 1985)
The Planets by Heather Couper (Franklin Watts, 1985)
The Planets by Michael Jay (Franklin Watts, 1982)
The Young Astronomer's Handbook by Ian Ridpath (Hamlyn, 1981)

Places to Visit

You can explore Uranus and other parts of the Universe without leaving Earth. Here are some places to visit.

Herschel House and Museum
19 New King Street, Bath

Science Museum
S. Kensington, London

Royal Observatory
Edinburgh, Scotland

Jodrell Bank Visitors' Centre
Macclesfield, Cheshire

London Planetarium
Marylebone Road,
London

Royal Greenwich Observatory
Herstmonceux Castle
Hailsham, E. Sussex

There are also planetaria at museums in Southend, Liverpool, National Maritime Museum (Greenwich, London), Armagh Observatory (N. Ireland), and Mills Observatory, Dundee (Scotland).

For More Information About Uranus

Here are some people you can write away to for more information about Uranus. Be sure to tell them exactly what you want to know about. And include your full name and address so they can write back to you.

About missions to Uranus:
NASA Kennedy Space Center
Educational Services Office
Kennedy Space Center, Florida 32899, USA

NASA Jet Propulsion Laboratory
Public Affairs 180-201
4800 Oak Grove Drive
Pasadena, California 91109, USA

For information about Uranus:
STARDATE
MacDonald Observatory
Austin, Texas 78712, USA

Glossary

atmosphere: the gases that surround a planet.

axis: the imaginary line through the centre of a planet around which the planet rotates. The axis of Uranus is tilted so that the planet appears to be on its side compared to the other planets in our Solar system.

billion: in this book, a billion means 1 followed by nine zeros i.e. 1,000,000,000 (a thousand million). A trillion means 1 followed by 12 zeros, i.e. 1,000,000,000,000 (a million million). These are standard figures in the United States and are becoming increasingly common in Britain, too. However, some other British books use the word billion to mean a million million. It is important to check which system a book is using.

'Bode's Law' : a formula that showed how far each planet should be from our Sun. First worked out by Daniel Titius, it later turned out to be false.

crater: a hole or pit in the ground caused by a volcanic explosion or by a meteor strike.

gravity: the force that causes objects like planets and their moons to be attracted to one another.

Herschel, William: a German astronomer who first discovered Uranus in 1781.

helium: a light, colourless gas that, along with hydrogen, makes up the atmosphere of Uranus.

mass: a quantity, or amount, of matter.

natural satellites: another name for the moons that orbit planets.

Oberon: one of the 15 moons of Uranus. Among the others are Titania, Ariel, and Miranda.

planet: one of the bodies that revolve around our Sun. Our Earth is one of the planets, and so is Uranus.

planetesimals: small bits of matter that, when joined together, may have formed planets.

radio telescope: an instrument that uses a radio receiver and antenna to both see into space and listen for messages from space.

rings: bits of matter that circle some planets, including Uranus.

space probes: satellites that travel in space, photographing celestial bodies and even landing on some of them. Voyager 1 and 2 are probes.

Umbriel: the darkest moon of Uranus.

Universe: everything we know that exists and believe may exist.

Uranus: a Greek god of the sky and the father of Saturn. The planet Uranus is named after him.

Voyager 2: the space probe that sent back valuable information about Uranus.

Index

The publishers wish to thank the following for permission to reproduce copyright material: front cover, pp. 8, 11, 16 (both), © Julian Baum; pp. 4, 7, 10, 14, 21, 23, 25 (upper), courtesy of NASA; p. 5 (upper), National Maritime Museum, hand-colored by Deborah Heinzel; p. 5 (lower), Royal Astronomical Society; pp. 9, 12, © David Hardy; pp. 15, 19, 20, 24, United States Geological Survey; p. 17, © Lynette Cook 1988; p. 22 (lower right), © MariLynn Flynn 1982; p. 22 (upper left), © MariLynn Flynn 1983; p. 25 (lower), © Alan Gutierrez 1979; p. 27, courtesy of Spaceweek National Headquarters; pp. 28-29, © Sally Bensusen.